BIRTHING *of* GREAT LEADERS

Birthing of Great Leaders

Copyright © 2017 Dr. David Ray Mathis, Sr., Th.D. All rights reserved.

No rights claimed for public domain material, all rights reserved. No parts of this publication may be reproduced, stored in any retrieval system, or transmitted in any form or by any means, electronic, mechanical, recording, or otherwise, without the prior written permission of the author. Violations may be subject to civil or criminal penalties.

Unless otherwise marked, all Scripture quotations are from the English Standard Version (ESV) The Holy Bible, English Standard Version Copyright © 2001 by Crossway Bibles, a publishing ministry of Good News Publishers and King James Version (KJV) by Public Domain.

Library of Congress Control Number: 2017934800

ISBN: 978-1-63308-259-5 (paperback)
978-1-63308-260-1 (ebook)

Interior and Cover Design by *R'tor John D. Maghuyop*

CHALFANT ECKERT
PUBLISHING

1028 S Bishop Avenue, Dept. 178
Rolla, MO 65401

Printed in United States of America

BIRTHING *of* GREAT LEADERS

Dr. David Ray Mathis, Sr., Th.D.

CHALFANT ECKERT
PUBLISHING

TABLE OF CONTENTS

Chapter 1:   Birthing of Great Leaders 7

Chapter 2:   The Womb of Man 13

Chapter 3:   Alone 27

Chapter 4:   Time 39

Chapter 5:   The Trying of Your Faith 43

Chapter 6:   Developing a Prayer Lifestyle 49

Chapter 7:   Spiritual Diet 53

Chapter 8:   Humility 57

Chapter 9:   Submission 61

Chapter 10:   Spiritual Control 67

Chapter 11:   PUSH! 73

References 77

CHAPTER 1

BIRTHING OF GREAT LEADERS

I want to discuss my topic the birthing of great leadership as a metaphor, because all great leaders have to endure the process. During a healthy pregnancy, there will be three trimesters, which will include nine months and nine different stages of development. Ecclesiastes 3:1-2 says:

> *For everything there is a season, and a time for every matter under heaven: a time to be born, and a time to die...*

There will be stages and seasons of processes in the life of those who are the chosen of God before the actual manifestation that will launch the leader into a place of great leadership.

The fruit of the Spirit (singular and inseparable) involves nine characteristics to describe God's perfect love:

> *But the fruit of the Spirit is love, joy, peace, patience, kindness, goodness, faithfulness, gentleness, self-control; against such things there is no law.*
> Galatians 5:22-23 (ESV)

Each of these must be tested in those who are placed in roles of great leadership. I chose to use nine stages because in each fruit there is a test to develop the heart and character of each leader. In each of the nine tests that a leader faces, he is not perfected but is given a more comprehensive understanding on how to walk in Godly integrity, thus reflecting the very nature of God.

The foundation of every great leader is built on the nine tests that he will have to endure over the course of his life, but God allows some tests to come after a leader is in a great leadership role to keep him humble. Everything in life must go through a diversified process, in essence, birthing, before it can be used. As individuals, God sees our potential, and He allows us to be challenged in areas that put immense pressure on our character. He does this to squeeze out the things which are not needed so that the things which are useable become evident and available for the Master to grow and strengthen us. The great pressure is not intended to kill us. It is intended to bring out the full potential of who we really are.

Jesus' life is a biblical example of how challenges develop and strengthen character. Hebrews 4:15 tells us:

> *For we do not have a high priest who is unable to sympathize with our weaknesses, but one who in every respect has been tempted as we are, yet without sin.*

Jesus was tested in every area just like we are. The test that really grabbed my attention was when Jesus was betrayed by someone who was in his inner circle (Judas).

> *Now the betrayer had given them a sign, saying, "The one I will kiss is the man; seize him." And he came up to Jesus at once and said, "Greetings, Rabbi!" And he kissed him.*
> Matthew 26:48-49 (ESV)

Not only was He betrayed, but the betrayal was sealed with a kiss from the lips of his disciple. I have observed that every person who has a great influence as a leader has endured betrayal from someone in his inner circle whom he or she loved dearly. I truly believe that betrayal is the birth canal that marks a higher level in ministry for any leader, but the leader must endure the betrayal without becoming bitter or vindictive.

Many may wonder why the birthing of great leadership occurs through great tests and trying times. God wants you to trust Him, He wants to trust you, and He wants you to succeed. That is why every person who has confessed Jesus Christ as Lord in their life will go through the birth canal of immense testing in life and trials. It is only through suffering that we learn to have a greater level of compassion for others that we would have otherwise misunderstood. Our compassion would have been less had we not gone through a season of trying times. You must recognize that trying times are a gift in the sense that they provide the environment for growth, the experiences to empower you to extend compassion to others, and even mentor those facing trying times.

Trying times also cultivates durability. Those times empower you to be unwavering and to maintain the position to which Christ has elevated you to become undeniably aware of who you are, who God is, and the gifts and callings of God on your life. The pain of trials in life are necessary for the birthing of great leadership because they help in the development of character so that you will become more productive as a leader in the Kingdom of God.

Many are the afflictions of the righteous,
but the Lord delivers him out of them all.
Psalm 34:19 (ESV)

Proverbs 3:11 urges us:

My son, do not despise the LORD's discipline
or be weary of his reproof

In the New Testament, Hebrews 5 tells us:

> *…My son, despise not thou the chastening of the Lord, nor faint when thou art rebuked of him: For whom the Lord loveth he chasteneth, and scourgeth every son whom he receiveth. If ye endure chastening, God dealeth with you as with sons; for what son is he whom the father chasteneth not? But if ye be without chastisement, whereof all are partakers, then are ye bastards, and not sons.*
> Hebrews 5:5-8 (ESV)

If you can endure rebuke, it shows maturity. When you endure the rebuke, correction, and instruction of God through mentors and your pastor,

> *The Lord will keep your going out and your coming in from this time forth and forevermore.*
> Psalm 121:8 (ESV)

No longer will you have to chase opportunity because enduring rebuke steadies and grounds you, develops trust, and shows what kind of mindset and character you have under pressure.

Before a tree produces a great yield of fruit, it must be pruned. Pruning is cutting back the branches so that the tree produces more fruit. Pruning also strengthens the tree to hold more fruit. As leaders, being able to take rebuke prunes you spiritually, giving you a greater capacity to bear more fruit. Pruning gives you wisdom as you come through the birth canal of different kinds of testing to become a great leader.

Tests are given for two purposes, to reveal your strengths, and to identify your weaknesses. The only way the core of your thought life can be empowered and grow is through the squeeze of great life tests. Great leaders must endure great testing of their thought lives before their thoughts can be reflected in reality.

Love will only grow through the test of joy, the test of peace, the test of long suffering, the test of gentleness, the test of goodness, the test of faith, the test of meekness, and the test of temperance. As each of these aspects of fruit of the Spirit is tested in your life, it produces layers of change. Similar to peeling back layers of an onion, the layers of testing begin to squeeze so tightly on the carnal mind that it looses its power, which causes love to sprout. God is love and love should be the core of your thought life.

The Bible uses many different analogies to describe the birthing of a masterpiece of God's creation: unrefined gold in the fire (1 Peter 1:7), clay on the potter's wheel (Jeremiah 18:3 and Isaiah 45:9), in the hand of the workman to make fine pottery (Jeremiah 18:4-6), grapes undergoing the squeeze of the winepress, and producing fine wine. Even Israel's beloved olive oil is made under the pressure of the olive press.

Before Jesus went to the cross, He went to pray at Gethsemane, which is at the foot of the Mount of Olives. The name Gethsemane is derived from the Aramaic term *Gaḏ-Šmānê,* meaning *oil press*. Jesus came to Earth as love wrapped in human flesh, but before love was reflected as love through Him, He experienced great pressure. The same applies to the development of your thought life, the great pressure you feel mentally at times is not intended to kill you, but to squeezes out the things that are not useful so that His love will be reflected in your life.

CHAPTER 2

THE WOMB OF MAN

Transformation starts in the mind.

Do not be conformed to this world, but be transformed by the renewal of your mind, that by testing you may discern what is the will of God, what is good and acceptable and perfect.
Romans 12:2 (ESV)

The Bible states:

For everything there is a season, and a time for every matter under heaven
Ecclesiastes 3:1 (ESV)

This is clearly evident in nature where you can see how time establishes cycles which bring forth the four seasons. Each season is different, but each will benefit the next. As Christians, we will go through different seasons of testing. Each season that you endure puts pressure on the core of your thought life causing your love for Christ to increase and become more potent. Similarly, when meat is marinated, each seasoning causes the meat to taste more like what it has been placed in. Having your thought life ruled by the Word of God is equivalent to a T-bone steak in your favorite marinade. However, the key to marinating is to know the perfect time to take the meat out. When it is grilled, baked, or stewed it will have the perfect amount of seasoning. In the same way, we must endure various seasons of trial. Enduring each season of testing intensifies and reflects the very nature of God, which is love.

> *Anyone who does not love does not know God, because God is love.*
> 1 John 4:8 (ESV)

The Core of Your Thought Life

If you understand anything about being a great athlete, then you know that it is of utmost importance to have good core strength, especially if you run track. The midsection or core is in the middle of your body. Everything has a core: the world, a peach, a foundation, even our spiritual being. When the core of any edifice is strong, the entire structure is stable. In the same way, a fruit can only be as healthy as its core. Your core muscles give you flexibility, power, and steadiness which are needed in every sport, professional or amateur. Love is the core of your thought life, it regenerates your thinking process and brings a transformation of the mind from a natural point of view to the spiritual realm giving you a spiritual understanding.

> *For to set the mind on the flesh is death,*
> *but to set the mind on the Spirit is life and peace.*
> Romans 8:6 (ESV)

Without love as the center of your thought life, you will become calloused with greed and lust, sinking deeper into carnality.

Love keeps the mind in a renewed state, not allowing it to become stagnant. Like a river flowing, the rocks and gravel keep the water clean and fresh. In the same way, the Word of God causes new life and brings transformation and new birth in your thought life.

In John 3:4, Nicodemus asked Jesus

How can a man be born when he is old?
Can he enter a second time into his mother's womb and be born?
John 3:4 (ESV)

Jesus always has an answer:

...Truly, truly, I say to you, unless one is born of water and the
Spirit, he cannot enter the kingdom of God. That which is born of
the flesh is flesh, and that which is born of the Spirit is spirit.
John 3:5-6 (ESV)

Water can be viewed as a cleaning agent because it is often used to wash or clean. Likewise, the Word of God is also a purging or cleaning agent that flushes out carnality. Therefore, it can be looked at as a symbol of the Holy Spirit, and only by the Holy Spirit can a mind be cultivated and altered to have compassion and make right choices based on the principles and Christ's Law of Love.

Nicodemus belonged to the Sanhedrin, the religious court in the time that Jesus walked among us. He was respected, one of few men given the power and trust to judge people and circumstances in the Jewish nation. He was an educated man with influence among his people. Yet, all that education and power could not give him salvation or cause him to exercise mercy and love. Only God's Word can accomplish that.

who has made us sufficient to be ministers
of a new covenant, not of the letter but of the Spirit.
For the letter kills, but the Spirit gives life.
II Corinthians 3:6 (ESV)

The mere letter of the Law of Moses was to produce a sense of guilt and danger, and not to produce pardon, relief, and joy. The law pronounced death, condemned sin in all forms, and the effect was to produce a sense of guilt and condemnation. But the Spirit gives life. The Spirit here seems to refer to the New Testament, or the new dispensation or inheritance, in contrast to the old. Living under the law was characterized mainly by its strictness and burdensome rites, and by the severe tone of its edict for sin. It did not in itself provide a way of pardon and peace.

Law condemns, it does not speak of forgiveness. On the contrary the gospel, a spiritual system providing mercy and forgiveness, is designed to impart life and comfort to the soul. It speaks peace. It comes not to condemn, but to save. It discloses a way of mercy, and it invites all to partake and live. Barnes (1947) stated, "It is called "spirit," probably because its consolations are imparted and secured by the Spirit of God - the source of all life to the soul. It is the dispensation of the Spirit; and it demands a spiritual service - a service that is free, and elevated, and tending eminently to purify the heart, and save the soul (p. 55).

As leaders, our effectiveness doesn't come from knowing the letter alone, but it is a combination of knowing the letter along with having the Spirit of God that brings our thought into the obedience of love. Every thought, vision, dream, and invention is born and developed in the mind, what I call *The Womb of Man*, before it becomes reality. Our faith and the foundation of our belief system are under constant attack from stress, doubt, fear, depression, low self-esteem and cause us to abort the plans that God has for our purpose and destiny.

> *Beloved, do not be surprised at the fiery trial when it comes upon*
> *you to test you, as though something strange were happening to you.*
> 1 Peter 4:12 (ESV)

It is a normal to experience thoughts that challenges the core of your thought life. To think otherwise can actually open the door for any of these negative thoughts to take root in the mind. Even Jesus' mind was challenged with negative thoughts beyond what we as mere humans could ever fathom.

The reason planets orbit the sun is that the gravity of the sun pulls on them and keeps them in their orbit. The sun keeps everything in space in order and all the planets draw strength from the sun. Just as the sun keeps all planets in order because of its gravitational pull, in the same way, the power of love is designed to keep every thought that comes to your mind in order with Christ's Law of Love.

> *for God gave us a spirit not of fear*
> *but of power and love and self-control*
> II Timothy 1:7 (ESV)

God didn't give us a spirit of fear so that it could manifest itself by fearful shrinking in daily difficulties. We as Christians meet difficulty in the warfare for the Kingdom of God with heavenly power, love, and a sound mindset to include self-control. The Holy Spirit works, in Christians and gives power to fight the fight of God, and also to strike good blows for Christ. This can be seen in steadfastness in resisting temptation and patience. Seeing mature Christians resist gives hope and guidance to weaker Christians as they find their Christian walk along the straight and narrow path of Godliness and love.

> *(For the weapons of our warfare are not carnal,*
> *but mighty through God to the pulling down of strong holds;)*
> *Casting down imaginations, and every high thing that exalteth*
> *itself against the knowledge of God, and bringing into captivity*
> *every thought to the obedience of Christ;*
> II Corinthians 10:4-5

Every thought that is not in alliance with love and every thought that doesn't revolve around love is a stronghold in seed form waiting to consume us, to bring our minds into bondage. We are not fighting a physical battle, even though at times it may look and feel that way. We are actually in spiritual warfare against inaccurate thought patterns that are designed to alter or sway the core of our thought life so as to drain us of any hope of being all we can be in Christ. Clarke and Smith (1875) stated, "The apostles often used the metaphor of warfare to represent the life and trials of a Christian minister." (p. 1334). We as ministers have three gateways in which the enemy can attack us to contaminate our minds: the eye gate, the mouth gate, and the ear gate.

> *A merry heart doeth good like a medicine:*
> *but a broken spirit drieth the bones.*
> Proverbs 17:22

The Gilead Institute of America describes it as:

Your mind and mental state can have a profound effect on your physical body, your spiritual experience, and your over-all quality of life. The mind, the body, and the spirit are all inextricably interconnected. When one is affected, the other two suffer. We can live a healthy lifestyle and perform our spiritual duties, but if the mind is not healthy the other two cannot make up for the lack, and we are not truly holistically healthy or healed.

Physical problems: Worry, anger, jealousy, hate, ill will, grudges, vindictiveness, irritation, resentment, guilt, depression, anxiety, lack of joy and happiness, and all other negative emotions and thoughts have a negative effect upon the body and open the door for sickness and disease.

(Your Mind Can Make You Sick, n.d.)

Negative thoughts have an effect on the mind like a *black hole*, which Wikipedia defines as a region of spacetime exhibiting such strong gravitational effects that nothing—not even particles and electromagnetic radiation such as light—can escape from inside it. The mind is full of space much like the real world and once a negative thought becomes more important than the power of love in your mind, it begins to pull with such force against the knowledge of truth that everything you see becomes negative. Once everyone appears to be negative, the negative thoughts turn on their hosts, pulling them into great depression.

Many shepherds are under extreme pressure because the weight of ministry is heavy and often there is no one to share problems with. An estimated 1,500 pastors throw in the towel and leave the ministry for other careers each month (Pastor Burnout, n.d.). Bleeding shepherds and bleeding leaders need people they can feel safe to share their struggles with. When your mind is sick or filled with nothing but negativity, then the whole body becomes ill. Rankin (2015) says it this way, "While many are aware of the seemingly mysterious placebo effect, fewer people know about its evil twin, 'the nocebo effect.'" She states that there is scientific proof that you can heal yourself. A combination of positive belief and the nurturing care of the right healer can activate the body's natural self–repair mechanisms and help the body heal itself.

Because the mind is the Womb of Man (the place where everything comes in seed form and vision and strategies are developed), the enemy always launches his greatest attacks in your mind. A carnal mind has no defense against the attack of the enemy because the carnal mind is at enmity with God:

> *Because the carnal mind is enmity against God: for it is not subject to the law of God, neither indeed can be.*
> Romans 8:7

Because we were born in sin, we are under two consistent attacks. One is with the carnal mind that cannot be subject to the Word of God, and the other attack is from people under Satan's influence, ordained to offset the timing of God to keep you from your purpose. Negative thoughts will come from your own psyche and from the lips of the people assigned by the enemy to hinder your destiny. These thoughts will work like rabies. Rabies is a viral disease that attacks the brain and spinal cord, or central nervous system. It's part of the Rhabdoviridae family of virus, under the genus Lyssavirus. The virus itself, like all members of Rhabdoviridae, is shaped like a bullet. Upon entering the body, it makes its way to the spinal cord via the peripheral nervous system afferent nerves (nerves that carry impulses toward the central nervous system once the virus gets into the spinal cord. It's quickly sent up to the brain, where it begins replicating itself inside the mind's nerve cells, destroying them in the process. After it reaches the brain, the virus typically travels through the different nerves (nerves that carry impulses away from the central nervous system) to the salivary glands, which often cause increased salivation or foaming at the mouth. It's important for the virus to do this, as this saliva is its principle method of transmission into other hosts. After hitting the salivary glands, the virus continues its way down throughout the rest of the body. Ephesians 6:16 states that the enemy will lunch fiery darts. These fiery darts are merely negative thoughts. Negative thoughts come from two places: demonic forces and negative people. If you receive negative words from the mouth of a negative person, it is equivalent to being bitten by a wild animal infected by the rabies virus.

> *Take us the foxes, the little foxes, that spoil the vines:*
> *for our vines have tender grapes.*
> Song of Solomon 2:15

Foxes are very cute animals with large appetites but are also destructive. When a fox takes fruit from a vine, it has no thought of saving the vine, but only filling its stomach. Negative thoughts work in the same way. A negative thought is programmed for one thing only, and that is negativity, so when a negative thought is entertained, it then reflects everything in reality as negative until everything you hear, see, and talk about becomes negative. Negative thoughts are like a vicious virus that attacks a computer. If it is not stopped it will eventually cause the computer to crash. Negative thoughts attack the core of your thought life as a Christian to stop the flow of the anointing on your life. It then begins to reproduce even more negative thoughts in your mind.

> *When the unclean spirit is gone out of a man, he walketh through*
> *dry places, seeking rest; and finding none, he saith, I will return*
> *unto my house whence I came out. And when he cometh, he findeth*
> *it swept and garnished. Then goeth he, and taketh to him seven*
> *other spirits more wicked than himself; and they enter in, and dwell*
> *there: and the last state of that man is worse than the first.*
> Luke 11:24-26

Like a Python squeezes its prey, the negative thoughts are designed to choke out faith in God. These negative thoughts then begin to spill out of the mouth of its host, causing death not only to the person that speaks them but to those who hear and allow the words to speak into their spirit.

> *Death and life are in the power of the tongue:*
> *and they that love it shall eat the fruit thereof.*
> Proverbs 18:21

We serve God in our minds and it is reflected by our actions which start from a thought formulated in the mind then spoken out of the mouth.

> *O generation of vipers, how can ye, being evil, speak good things?*
> *for out of the abundance of the heart the mouth speaketh.*
> Matthew 12:34

You can't control the thoughts that come through your mind, but you can control what you meditate on.

> *This book of the law shall not depart out of thy mouth; but thou*
> *shalt meditate therein day and night, that thou mayest observe to do*
> *according o all that is written therein: for then thou shalt make thy*
> *way prosperous, and then thou shalt have good success.*
> Joshua 1:8

Often when we experience hurtful situations, our carnal minds want to respond in carnal ways. The mind begins to meditate on how it will respond to the problem. When this happens, the Word of God will come to mind immediately. This is when we decide if we will give in to our carnal nature or follow the voice of God.

> *The steps of a good man are ordered by the Lord:*
> *and he delighteth in his way.*
> Psalm 37:23

This verse is often quoted in terms of the direction in which a Christian is taking without referring to where the directions came from, but the steps of a good man are ordered by the Word of God and the course of his life is shifted into the path in which God has ordained him to walk in. The thoughts of a good man are ordered by the Lord to keep him in peace in the midst of spiritual warfare.

Every vision is formed in our minds. We experience reasoning, feelings, emotions, and insight. Our imaginations and creativity have roots in our brains, and every action we take is preceded by a corresponding thought. The mind is the womb of man, the place where a thought is like a seed, and that seed can become a vision which grows and makes provision for billions of others.

P. K. Bernard said, "A man without vision is a man without a future. A man without a future will always return to his past." (Power of a Vision, n.d.) Vision is the bridge between the present and the future. Without it we perish or go "unrestrained," as the New American Standard Bible puts it (Proverbs 29:18). Vision gives pain a purpose. Those without vision spend their lives taking the path of least resistance as they try to avoid discomfort. The level of sacrifice that a vision requires will determine the size of who follows that vision. Willingness to sacrifice separates the immature and selfish from spiritually mature Christians. No one becomes great outwardly before he first become great in his mind.

A vision from God is developed by love to sustain life and bring hope to the hopeless. As the Word of God begins to transform the mind, the vision inside you begins to grow, and through each failure that you endure, your compassion for others intensifies. The pain and struggles that you experience in life are not for you, but intertwined in every affliction that you endure is the blueprint for the vision that God has placed in your heart. Without the experiences of struggle, the vision that's in your mind could never be birthed.

> *For our light affliction, which is but for a moment, worketh for us a*
> *far more exceeding and eternal weight of glory*
> II Corinthians 4:17

Romans 8 tells us that depression, distress, persecution and all real and imagined threats are fashioned to work for the good of them that love the Lord and are called according to his purpose.

The Importance of Having a Clear Mind and Healthy Womb

Having a clear mind is equivalent to having a healthy womb because both must be in a clear and healthy state before birth or productivity will take place.

> *He that hath an ear, let him hear what the*
> *Spirit saith unto the churches; To him that overcometh will*
> *I give to eat of the hidden manna, and will give him a white stone,*
> *and in the stone a new name written, which no man*
> *knoweth saving he that receiveth it.*
> Revelation 2:17

When your thoughts are clouded with negativity, it's like leaving a door cracked for past habits to creep back into your life. A clear mind is like a clear night sky; you can see whatever you need to see with the natural eye or through a telescope. However, a cloudy sky is like a mind filled with chaos. A clear mind can only be obtained through continual study of the Word of God and prayer. Remembering and repeating this verse will help in clearing your mind,

> *For God hath not given us the spirit of fear;*
> *but of power, and of love, and of a sound mind.*
> II Timothy 1:7

You must cast down every thought of fear and walk in faith guided by the Holy scriptures.

> *Howbeit when he, the Spirit of truth, is come,*
> *he will guide you into all truth: for he shall not speak of himself;*
> *but whatsoever he shall hear, that shall he speak:*
> *and he will shew you things to come.*
> John 16:13

The Word of God is there to guide you and help you keep your focus but it will never condemn you or cause you to lose hope. You can't allow yourself to entertain negative thoughts because negative thoughts are the offspring of demonic forces designed by Satan to take root in your mind and choke out faith-filled words and scriptures.

> *And these are they which are sown among thorns;*
> *such as hear the word, And the cares of this world, and the*
> *deceitfulness of riches, and the lusts of other things entering in,*
> *choke the word, and it becometh unfruitful.*
> Mark 4:18-19

There can be no productivity if the mind is full of negativity. We serve a God that is ever evolving, but never changing, who left an example for us to have a singleness of heart concerning the things of His Kingdom.

> *Jesus Christ the same yesterday, and to day, and for ever.*
> Hebrews 13:8

We serve a triune God who is not subject to our human limitations. He is omnipresent and though He is God the Father, God the Son, and God the Holy Spirit, yet is He one God having a mind that is united.

> *Hear, O Israel: The Lord our God is one Lord:*
> Deuteronomy 6:4

You can't separate any part of who God is. Neither can His Word be altered, it is forever settled in heaven and it cannot be broken, including His grace, His sovereignty, His love and His mercy. In order to reflect on who Christ is, you first must have His Word written upon the table of your heart.

Therefore shall ye lay up these my words in your heart and in your soul, and bind them for a sign upon your hand, that they may be as frontlets between your eyes.
Deuteronomy 11:18

God's Word is designed to ground you against the ongoing flood of damnable doctrines that will come to corrupt your mind. Other doctrines and beliefs come in like a flood against the knowledge of truth that has been planted in your psyche and heart.

So shall they fear the name of the Lord from the west, and his glory from the rising of the sun. When the enemy shall come in like a flood, the Spirit of the Lord shall lift up a standard against him.
Isaiah 59:19

I have never heard of a woman having two wombs, but I have heard of a woman having twins which came from one womb. We were created with one mind so it's important to keep a clear thought life, both naturally and spiritually, so that we can perform whatever task is given to us by almighty God with accuracy and excellence.

CHAPTER 3

ALONE

My life was very strange as a young man. I can remember walking through the woods praying near my home in Hope, Arkansas. I was about eight or nine years old when my father, the late James Ray Mathis, passed away. He was a great singer and young pastor and I wanted to be just like him. Facing the loss of my father was one of the greatest challenges of my life, and as a young man, very hard to overcome. After my father died, my mother began pastoring a small church in Bradley, Arkansas. I can recall crying many days after my father passed away because I missed him so deeply. His absence created a wound in my heart that it took me many years to work through. At nine years old, I can remember walking through the woods with tears in my eyes praying, asking God to help me and telling Him that I wanted to preach and sing like my father. I didn't realize that every tear that fell from my face was watering my dream. Likewise, my brothers and sisters in Christ, I know you may have cried and may still be crying, but every tear you shed is watering your dream. Keep crying, but don't stop pursuing your dreams. Stop trying to make people believe in a dream that God has given you. Understand this: No one will ever see in you what God has shown you about your destined place in His kingdom. Only you can see it, so don't stop pursuing!

One evening while walking in the woods of Hope, Arkansas, I heard a voice say, "You will be a pastor." I can remember looking up at the sky in amazement because of what I had just heard. At that time, I had never preached before, but about two weeks later, the pastor from Hope, Arkansas, allowed about fifteen young men to speak at his church. I was among the fifteen. He gave each of us about five minutes on a Sunday morning. That was the longest five minutes of my life, I thought, and I preached from Proverbs 3:1-3. No one helped me with what to say. No one told me what chapter to preach from but when I opened my Bible, it came alive to me. At that point I really began to read the Bible as much as possible and I prayed every day. But I still felt like I was alone. When I turned thirteen years old, I wanted to work in the town where my father had pastored. That was about fifty miles from our home. My mother allowed me to stay in our old church in Bradley, Arkansas, during the summer months to work because she knew the contractor. I read my Bible and prayed every night. Some nights I was afraid because the building was old and I could hear it popping and cracking. Alone in the dark, God began to deal with me and show me dreams. That made me more afraid because I had a dream I didn't understand. I told our senior pastor, and he asked me to share it with the church. Two weeks later the dream came to pass. In the dream, I saw a tornado destroy a home and then it went into another home which subsequently exploded like sawdust. It happened just as I had seen it in my dream. One house was destroyed because a huge tree was pushed down by the tornado-force winds, but the other house wasn't hit by a physical storm. It was hit by a spiritual storm and the couple who lived there divorced and never reconciled. My senior pastor and my father were good friends so the pastor took me under his wing and gave me all that he could as a man. But I still felt a deep loneliness inside because I was still grieving over my father's death. At thirteen I began to preach at many of our youth conferences, but I still felt alone. The Lord was teaching me a lesson. I just got the revelation that every leader experiences loneliness in a way that no one else can understand.

The birthing of great leadership is a personal event because it doesn't start by our actions but it is first developed in our thought lives. Then like a cup that's overfilled with water, it is reflected in our actions from day to day. We as humans are all seeds. However, a seed must fall into the ground and die but during its death will experience a great deal of isolation and loneliness. While in the ground, a seed appears limited. It appears stunted by the ground surrounding it, but underneath the pressure of the ground pushing down on it, the seed is drawing life from something that seems worthless (dirt). As bad as it may seem or appear, we all need a little dirt on us to help us grow. That dirt can take the form of obstacles to overcome, health issues to endure, or people turning against us.

> *Blessed are ye, when men shall revile you, and persecute you,*
> *and shall say all manner of evil against you falsely, for my sake.*
> Matthew 5:11

When a seed is conceived, it will be alone for nine months in the dark of the mother's womb going through various transformations. It transforms into an embryo with the brain, spinal cord, and heart. Then the legs begin to form. Later the fetus develops all the major organs and his or her external body structures such as arms, legs, eyelids, and face. Then the baby's structure further develops until all systems are operational and fully developed and the skin is intact also. We as leaders are like a seed in a womb and it is part of our destiny to spend a great deal of our lives alone.

Alone is where growth takes place, it's also where development of Christian character and mental metamorphous takes place in the mind of His chosen.

> *Verily, verily, I say unto you,*
> *Except a corn of wheat fall into the ground and die, it abideth*
> *alone: but if it die, it bringeth forth much fruit.*
> John 12:24

The seed loses its original form and the outer shell has to break off so that new life can spring forth.

> *For if we have been planted together in the likeness of his death,*
> *we shall be also in the likeness of his resurrection:*
> Romans 6:5

Growing hurts, it doesn't feel good to go through or endure some of the things that we do as sons of God.

Thou therefore endure hardness, as a good soldier of Jesus Christ.
II Timothy 2:3

When something dies, it starts to decay, shifting from its original form. Things then began to break off and everything begins to decompose until there is nothing left but bone, whether an animal or human. But if it's a piece of fruit it will rot down to the seed. When God allows you alone time, He intends for things to break off. He wants you to shift from your original form into the vessel that He desires you to be for the nations. So, what does God do? He plants you in an environment that is conducive to your destination, an environment that challenges you according to the path you will soon walk in as a leader. It is the alone time and pressure of being underneath that prepares the seed to feed the masses. It is in your alone time that you develop and receive the directions needed for your life to fulfill what has be spoken over you through a dream, vision, or through a prophet of God that has spoken over your life. If you use the time that God has granted you wisely, you also learn about your gift and how to flow in your gifting to create a consecrated lifestyle. It takes time to become who God wants you to be, but God will often plant you in the problem so that you can be resurrected as a part of the solution.

Joseph had a dream. He said,

For, behold, we were binding sheaves in the field, and, lo, my sheaf arose, and also stood upright; and, behold, your sheaves stood round about, and made obeisance to my sheaf.
Genesis 37:7

After Joseph told his brothers the dream, they hated him. Joseph had another dream and in this dream,

…the sun, the moon, and eleven stars were bowing down to me.
Genesis 37:9 (ESV)

When Joseph told his father the dream, Jacob reprimanded him, and his brothers hated him even more. He was the favored son of the twelve, so there was already animosity between the siblings. This seething anger his brothers felt would play a role in God's plan, but neither the brothers or Jacob knew that God would use Joseph's dream to create the events necessary to grow Joseph into his future. Through the dream, God gave Joseph a glimpse of the future that his family did not understand or even like.

No one can see what God has shown you about your future, they can only see the outer shell of an unfinished product. When a caterpillar goes through metamorphosis you can only see the outer casing of the cocoon. You don't know what will emerge. You don't know what color it will be, but it will come out with a major change. In the same way, you will come out of your metamorphosis totally different than anyone can imagine.

God gave Noah the vision to build the ark. No one could understand what he was doing,

> *Make thee an ark of gopher wood; rooms shalt thou make in the ark, and shalt pitch it within and without with pitch.*
> Genesis 6:14

Can you imagine the ridicule Noah and his family put up with? For years, he worked on a huge ocean-worthy vessel the size of an aircraft carrier in the middle of the desert. He warned his neighbors that God would send a great flood and it would rain for forty days and nights. How they must have scoffed and laughed at him! There had never been rain on the earth before, and here was this old man proclaiming a flood. They must have thought he was nuts. Even when the animals came to the ark, they looked on in wonder but not one soul got on the ark before God closed the door. They could not see Noah's vision.

Whenever God gives you a vision of who you are and what you will do in the future, people can't see beyond who you are now. There are two reasons why I believe many people can't see the vision God has given you about your life. The first is that you enter into what I call *the hiding*, and second is that you will enter into the process designed especially for you until He decides the season is right to launch your ministry and you will remain hidden in what appears to be difficult times for you as a leader, whether *being hidden* or *being processed* by God's divine hand of protection.

> *He that dwelleth in the secret place of the most*
> *High shall abide under the shadow of the Almighty. I will say of the*
> *Lord, He is my refuge and my fortress: my God; in him will I trust.*
> *Surely he shall deliver thee from the snare of the fowler, and from*
> *the noisome pestilence.*
> Psalm 91:1-3

Often when your enemy has laid a trap for you and it appears to them that you are trapped, it's only a decoy so that God can get the glory out of what appears to be a bad situation. What appears to be a trap may be a part of God's plan to protect you.

> *But as for you, ye thought evil against me; but God meant it unto*
> *good, to bring to pass, as it is this day, to save much people alive.*
> Genesis 50:20

The many letters that Apostle Paul wrote from prison were in God's plan to protect him. It could very well have been that someone during that time had set up an evil plot to kill Apostle Paul. The time of hiding and the time of process are stages in which we may feel very isolated as a leader, but this alone time is necessary to be ready to reach your final destination in the Kingdom of God.

> *And the woman conceived, and bare a son: and when she saw him*
> *that he was a goodly child, she hid him three months.*
> Exodus 2:2

It was designed by God that Moses be hidden and processed for a season to protect him until the season was right. When God gives you a vision of your destiny in the Kingdom, He then allows afflictions and naysayers to cross your path. The afflictions are to help you deal with the weight of ministry because ministry at times can be weighty on many levels.

> *For our light affliction, which is but for a moment, worketh for us a far more exceeding and eternal weight of glory;*
> II Corinthians 4:17

> *And it came to pass, when Moses held up his hand, that Israel prevailed: and when he let down his hand, Amalek prevailed. But Moses hands were heavy; and they took a stone, and put it under him, and he sat thereon; and Aaron and Hur stayed up his hands, the one on the one side, and the other on the other side; and his hands were steady until the going down of the sun.*
> Exodus 17:11-12

Naysayers are those who will drop a negative seed in your ear to discourage you the moment they get the opportunity, or cause you to disbelieve the word that God has spoken over your life. In other words, they are on an assignment by the enemy to detour you from your destiny. Joseph heard negativity and ridicule from his own family after he told them the dream that God showed him. Joseph went out to meet his brothers, but when they saw him from a distance, they plotted to kill him. When Joseph made it to where his brothers were, they ripped off his coat and threw him into a pit. Joseph's journey began in the pit that his brothers threw him in but while he was in the pit he could hear his brothers conspiring against him. Often God will allow you to experience a low place in life to teach you humility, but while you are in your pit, He will allow you to hear the naysayers planning your demise, but intertwined in their evil plot to kill you is knitted your victory. While their brother was still in the pit, Joseph' siblings saw a caravan of merchants in the distance and decided to sell Joseph. Instead of killing him, they sold him for twenty pieces of silver because they didn't want the blood on their hands. Joseph's brothers knew how much their father loved Joseph, so to cover their tracks, they took Joseph's coat of many colors that Jacob had made for him, killed a kid and dipped the coat in the blood. When Jacob saw Joseph's blood-drenched coat, he wept and wailed thinking a wild animal had killed his beloved son.

The coat that Joseph wore was something that his father had made specially for him, and it represented favor. I brought this point out because the first thing your haters want to do when they see the favor of God on your life is figure out a way to stain your integrity with scandal. But every evil plot and snare that the enemy has designed for you to fall into is part of the plan that God uses to show that He is with you. When looking at the story of Joseph, after he was sold, it appeared to be over for his life. He was sold into slavery, but it was a setup of future events by God to make sure Joseph was in the right place at the right time to interpret Pharaoh's dream. God gave Joseph dreams and the gift of interpreting other's dreams. There are some things that will happen in your life that are just out of your control, but what appears a hopeless situation to you could well be part of God's plan to bring you into a great inheritance to save or influence many lives for the Kingdom of God.

> [12] *Beloved, think it not strange concerning the fiery trial which is to try you, as though some strange thing happened unto you:*
> [13] *But rejoice, inasmuch as ye are partakers of Christ's sufferings; that, when his glory shall be revealed, ye may be glad also with exceeding joy.*
> I Peter 4:12-13

While Joseph was working as Potiphar's slave, God was with him and Joseph found favor in the eyes of Potiphar. The more responsibility Potiphar gave Joseph, the more the Lord blessed Joseph and Potiphar's household. While looking at Joseph's story, you almost forget that he was a slave because God blessed everything Joseph touched. Alone in Egypt working as a slave, slowly Joseph began to experience promotion. He was loyal to his master, but Potiphar's wife was uncontrollably attracted to Joseph. Joseph was a young man and this attraction put him in a difficult position. He knew that his master's wife wanted to be with him so he tried to avoid her. But working full time as a slave, how could he? When the house was empty, she would throw herself at Joseph and he would flee. One day when the house was empty, the snare was set. Potiphar's wife wasn't taking no for an answer so she grabbed his robe. Joseph ran out of the house without his robe. He ran out with his integrity, he ran out with his character, and he ran out with his loyalty. Potiphar's wife was angry and accused him of trying to rape her. He was sent to prison for about two years until Pharaoh had a dream which needed to be interpreted. Joseph had God's gifting to interpret the dream for Pharaoh, and he was let out prison and made second in command in the land of Egypt.

Every event that happened in Joseph's life was set for God to get the glory, while also giving Joseph the foundation and experience that he needed for his future. Every event that appeared to be a trap to take his life and freedom was actually the alone time that God wanted Joseph to have so that he would be in the right position and his gift could make room for him.

A man's gift maketh room for him,
and bringeth him before great men.
Proverbs 18:16

When you are hidden behind the slanders and lies, when you are the new kid on the block and no one knows who you are and you are looked at like as an outsider, know this: It is a miracle in the making. I believe Joseph felt and came to understand that he was in the palm of God's hand, protected and cared for even when he was alone. You must endure all these things that take place in your life in your alone time because they are the perfect ingredients to make your gift blossom. Your alone time is the opportunity that you have been waiting for, seize it and use it for God's glory.

My brethren, count it all joy when ye fall into divers temptations;
Knowing this, that the trying of your faith worketh patience.
James 1:2-3

I have endured great trials and tests in becoming the leader God wants me to be. I have been an armor-bearer. I was the janitor, I kept the grass cut and the church clean. I was a musician and part of the praise and worship team. I was an evangelist and teacher and received no pay for anything I did. I share that because I want you to realize that you must be flexible. Now over twenty years later, God is rewarding me for things that I did willingly in my past years.

If ye be willing and obedient, ye shall eat the good of the land:
Isaiah 1:19

Your flexibility helps to ensure that you are a well-rounded leader, not only knowing how to lead but also having the ability to mentor those that come alongside you. You must keep a servant's heart and a teachable attitude. These are keys in your process of developing as a leader. Joseph had the heart of a servant so God was able to use him in many different positions which prepared him to be Pharaoh's second-in-charge leader.

But Jesus called them to him, and saith unto them,
Ye know that they which are accounted to rule over the Gentiles
exercise lordship over them; and their great ones
exercise authority upon them.
⁴³ But so shall it not be among you: but whosoever
will be great among you, shall be your minister: And whosoever of
you will be the chiefest, shall be servant of all. For even the Son of
man came not to be ministered unto, but to minister,
and to give his life a ransom for many.
Mark 10:42-45

When Moses was just an infant, his mother discerned that he was a good child and hid him from the persecution of Pharaoh for three months.

By faith Moses, when he was born, was hid three months of his
parents, because they saw he was a proper child; and they were not
afraid of the king's commandment.
Hebrews 11:23

Isolation is lonely and not a place that most leaders want to be but without a period of alone time, you would not have time to perfect your craft. When his mother couldn't hide Moses anymore, she built him an ark of bulrushes and pitched it with slime and put him in the river. She knew that Pharaoh's daughter and handmaidens would be in the river. When Pharaoh's daughter saw the child, her heart was filled with compassion. She took the child as her own and paid the child's mother to continue to nurse him, not knowing it was Moses' real mother she had hired.

And the child grew, and she brought him unto Pharaoh's daughter, and he became her son. And she called his name Moses: and she said, Because I drew him out of the water.
Exodus2 :10

God knows how to protect you and where to protect you, while at the same time giving you the tools required for the assignment on your life. God's plot was set skillfully to hide Moses behind enemy walls so that he could learn the ways of the Egyptians and understand Pharaoh's vicious heart. One day Moses was out walking and saw the hard labor of his people. In the distance, he saw an Egyptian beating a Hebrew man. Moses went into a rage and killed the Egyptian and hid the body in the sand. When Pharaoh found out what had occurred, Moses had to flee. Moses met Zipporah while running from Pharaoh, and she later became his wife. God taught Moses humility through tending his father-in-law's sheep.

Before God raises you up, He will bring you to a place of great humility. Humility is a strong foundation. It also reminds you of the place that God brought you, the humble places you endured, and teaches you necessary compassion as you mentor the next generation. Alone Moses tended the sheep for forty years. A lot of negative thoughts probably went through his mind. God had to take him through those forty years to teach him humility. Forty years is a long time so he could have felt worthless, as if it was a waste of his time. But God was molding Moses into the leader that He wanted him to be. God was preparing him to deal with the physical elements and realities of life in the desert where he would spend forty years with the murmuring Israelites. God also taught Moses to go before the most powerful man in all the land, the Egyptian Pharaoh.

Only God knows what circumstances and challenges you will face as a leader. He will put you in situations that will exert immense pressure to prepare you for your chosen purpose. It is in times of isolation that transformation takes place. I want to encourage you not to despise your alone time. It is the time when no one has discovered or knows who you are. It may be the only vacation you will ever get again! Once you are in a leadership role, it will take time to work as an effective and productive leader. Moses had forty years of isolation to prepare him for forty years of dealing with a group of stubborn, stiff-necked people who caused Moses frustration and thus caused him to miss the Promised Land.

Use your alone time to get to know the Lord, become a student of the Word of God, and set aside a time to get in the presence of the Lord daily so that when your appointed time comes to be on the front lines, you will be able to walk into the promised land with God's people and not look from a distance like Moses did.

CHAPTER 4

TIME

Time plays an important role in the birthing of a great leader. From the beginning until now, time has always played an immense part in God's creation. All things went through the process of time. We see this as true through various examples in the Bible. In Genesis 1, we see that God took six days to create the heavens and the earth though He could have spoken one word and the earth would have come into existence. God took time to develop the heavens and the earth, plants, animals, and man, one day at a time for six days. Even after the fall of man, God developed a redemption that came to fruition with the passage of time through the propitiation or substitutionary death of Christ.

It takes time to become a great leader. Just like baking a cake takes time: gathering the right ingredients, mixing them just right, and most importantly, allowing the cake to bake completely. In the same way, the process of becoming a great leader also takes time. If God takes you out of the process too early, it would be like a cake taken out too early, you will be undercooked. If you stay in the process too long, you would be overdone. God knows when you are ready, how much you can take, and when to pull you out. This plays a vital part in the process of your becoming a great leader.

There hath no temptation taken you but such as is common to man: but God is faithful, who will not suffer you to be tempted above that ye are able; but will with the temptation also make a way to escape, that ye may be able to bear it.
I Corinthians 10:13

Being faced with trials and tests gives us the assurance that we are right where God wants us to be and our deliverance will come at the right time. We endure the trials God sets up for us even though it may feel as though it takes longer for people and less time for others. The timing is necessary in the development of great leaders, so that we are seasoned ministers of God, able to rightly divide the Word of Truth so that our words will be tasteful to those we teach. God's timing is often difficult for today's carnal mind to receive because advancements and technology have spoiled our generation, we want everything immediately. You now can cook oatmeal in 60 seconds, get prescription glasses in 60 minutes, and build a house in 60 days. This is a generation hardwired to speeds not available in previous generations so when God doesn't move in their desired timing, many disbelieve that there is a sovereign God and that He is able to do exceedingly and abundantly above all you can ask or think (Ephesians 3:20). God moves in His timing, not ours. He is looking for maturity, not speed. Thus, impatience causes many to miss God's perfect timing. I have seen in my walk with God many men and women who moved out of the timing of God and established churches that started out as storefront churches and thirty years later are still in the same storefront. It is important to learn from nature, the whole earth is built on time, seasons, and cycles: morning, noon, night, winter, spring, summer, and fall. But between every cycle and season is time.

A friend of mine explains how we experience time in this way: We will all be touched by and experience the passage of time before we leave this earth. People experience time differently at different points in their life cycles. Young people are impatient and can't wait to grow up. Waiting for next year's birthday party seems like it takes forever to arrive. That is because for a year to pass in the life of a five-year-old child, twenty percent of his or her life must come to pass for that birthday to arrive. As people get older, time speeds up. Waiting for the next birthday for a fifty-year-old man only takes up two percent of his life, so it goes by much faster. Can you imagine in the days of Methuselah how fast a year must have seemed once someone was five hundred years old? A year would have been one fifth of one percent of the person's life! Bickford, K. (2017, February 15). Personal interview.

Luke 5:1-11 tells us that Peter was an expert fisherman and tells of a night when they had toiled for many hours and caught nothing. Because of the kind of fishing they were doing, it had to be done at night so the fish wouldn't see their nets. Jesus was passing through at the break of day and saw their boats were empty. They were mending their nets getting ready for the next night but Jesus told Peter to launch out into the deep and let down his nets. Peter being an expert fisherman and aware of the timings told Jesus that they had toiled all night but had caught nothing. However, Peter (also called Simon) responded thusly:

And Simon answering said unto him, Master,
we have toiled all the night, and have taken nothing:
nevertheless at thy word I will let down the net.
Luke 5:5

Peter could have let his expertise rob him of a great blessing. When he let down his net, he caught many fish. This account shows how different God's timing is from our timing and the importance of obeying God. Don't move out of God's timing and away from the instructions of your leader.

But let patience have her perfect work,
that ye may be perfect and entire, wanting nothing.
James 1:4

CHAPTER 5

THE TRYING OF YOUR FAITH

Hebrews 11:6 tells us that without faith, it is impossible to please God. Faith in the Word of God is difficult for the human mind to comprehend because the human mind was designed to understand things through the five senses (touch, taste, hearing, smell, and sight). Before a leader can be considered a great leader, his faith in God must be tried in the eyes of his community so that God can get the glory from what appears to be total disaster.

The Bible describes our carnal mind like this:

Because the carnal mind is enmity against God: for it is not subject to the law of God, neither indeed can be.
Romans 8:7

Despite this, without faith it is impossible to please God. Thus, we must grow in faith if we desire to become great leaders in the Kingdom of God. The Bible teaches that faith comes by hearing and hearing by the Word of God (Romans 10:17). We as believers must be students of the Word of God, constantly studying and seeking God's guidance to build up our inner man, just as an athlete constantly trains and exercises to develop and build inner strength and endurance. As you continue to read and study the Word of God, your understanding is enlightened, revelation is given which increases your faith, and the transforming effect that takes place in your mind will begin to show that development has taken place in your faith according to the Word of God. By studying and by building a proper relationship with God steeped in the Word and prayer, a person moves from being controlled by his or her carnal mind to being controlled by the Spirit of God through God's Word.

Once we believe God, we then grow in character and our faith grows through tests and trials. Abraham believed God, and it was counted as righteousness in God's eyes (Genesis 15:6). God asked Abram to leave his home and go to a land he barely knew, where God would make Abram and his descendants into a great nation. In faith, he gathered his flock and his wife and went as God had asked. The first test of faith that Abram experienced was the test of leaving his country and his kindred and his father's house to go to a land that God would show him (Genesis 12:1). While on his journey with God, he almost lost his wife to the King of Egypt and was betrayed by and almost lost his kinsman (Lot), but his faith in God grew with every trial because as he believed God, God showed up in His perfect time. God changed his name from Abram to Abraham to signify that he would be the father of many nations. In Abraham's physical reality, he was old and childless. God also changed Sarai's name to Sarah which meant *princess*. As time passed, Abraham's spirit was heavy because he was seventy-five years old and had no heir; he had not received the promise. His wife was stricken in age too, but Abraham kept the faith and this pleased God. When he was a hundred years old, and his wife was ninety, they received the promised child (Genesis 21:2). After they had received the promised child, God gave Abraham a final test, the greatest test of his life. He asked Abraham to give back to Him the promised child, the son that Abraham had waited for so long and finally received, the very Isaac from whom the many nations would spring from (Genesis 22:2). In faith, Abraham obeyed God.

> *And Abraham said, My son, God will provide himself a lamb for a burnt offering: so they went both of them together.*
> Genesis 22:8

Abraham raised the knife to slay his son, Isaac, but God showed up through an angel and stopped the sacrifice. Then God provided a ram in the bush, providing his own sacrifice just as Abraham had said in faith. Abraham's mind must have been under great pressure, but he kept the faith, focusing on the promise and not on the circumstances.

The trying of your faith is designed to build and increase your faith. Through Abraham's testing, he was viewed as the father of many nations and the father of faith because he endured. Job is another outstanding example of faith. Job held onto his integrity despite losing everything he had: wealth, family, friends and even his health. Throughout and at the end of his trial, Job's faith in God and his character became established and intact.

> *Though he slay me, yet will I trust in him: but I will maintain mine own ways before him.*
> Job 13:15

He held steadfast to his belief and to his God:

> *I have heard of thee by the hearing of the ear: but now mine eye seeth thee.*
> Job 42:5

Job's latter years were greater than his former years because he was tried and found to be faithful, so God entrusted him with more than he had at the beginning. God knew even with much that Job would remain faithful.

God tests and tries us and puts us on his potter's wheel to shape and form us into spiritual vessels needed to do His work on earth.

> *Then I went down to the potter's house, and, behold, he wrought a work on the wheels.*
> Jeremiah 18:3

God's hands develop us into the leaders He desires. After clay has been shaped into a vessel and dried, the potter places the vessel into a kiln where it is subjected to intense heat (about 1,750° F.) for about a day. The process is called "firing" and it changes the clay's malleable form to one that is durable and can stand time and weathering. In the Qumran caves, pottery vessels containing the Dead Sea Scrolls were still intact. The scrolls were originally written between about a hundred years before and after Christ and placed in earthen clay vessels. Those vessels survived for thousands of years because they went through the fiery process to harden them and make them strong. There is a parallel in the Bible between the firing of clay and the fiery trials of humans.

Beloved, think it not strange concerning the fiery trial which is to try you, as though some strange thing happened unto you: But rejoice, inasmuch as ye are partakers of Christ's sufferings; that, when his glory shall be revealed, ye may be glad also with exceeding joy.
I Peter 4:12-13

Great leaders must endure great trials as the Lord takes them from glory to glory. A vessel (individual) must go through the fire to be hardened, strengthening God's chosen vessel so that he or she can be used to the glory of God.

Similarly, 1 Peter 1:6-7 tells us

Wherein ye greatly rejoice, though now for a season, if need be, ye are in heaviness through manifold temptations: ⁷ That the trial of your faith, being much more precious than of gold that perisheth, though it be tried with fire, might be found unto praise and honour and glory at the appearing of Jesus Christ:

After the vessel comes through the intense heat and does not crack, it is pleasing to the potter. We are the clay pot in the kiln, and the heat represents the trials and tests we face in which we must endure until we develop into the form that God wants for us. The trying of our faith will take us to new levels of glory but with every level will come a different degree of trials and testing. As we endure various degrees of trials, our faith is strengthened. The process of becoming a great leader never happens until we embrace the Word of God in its entirety and thus grow strong faith in God. We will go through many trials in our walk with God to ready us for what God has planned for us. Before God can trust us or bring increase, our character must develop through the trying of our faith until we are ready.

CHAPTER 6

DEVELOPING A PRAYER LIFESTYLE

Hananiah, Mishael, Azariah, and Belteshazzar (better known as Shadrach, Meshach and Abednego, and Daniel) were taken captive by King Nebuchadnezzar. Daniel served in prominent positions in the government during that time. He was faithful to God praying three times a day. King Nebuchadnezzar had a dream that the Chaldeans and Babylonian soothsayers could not interpret. The king was angry and was going to kill every wise man if one of them didn't interpret his dream. Daniel didn't even ask what the dream was about, the first thing Daniel did was call his prayer partners (Shadrack, Meshach, and Adednego) to pray. It was through prayer that God revealed the interpretation of King Nebuchadnezzar's dream.

God will reveal things that are hidden from you through prayer.

Pray without ceasing.
I Thessalonians 5:17

It may seem impossible to pray without ceasing, but it can be done in the form of mediating, praising, and worshiping. You can pray around friends and family, and mediate in your heart among strangers. Regardless of physical posture, whether praying prostrate, on bended knee, with head bowed, or speaking out loud to God, prayer is so powerful that it changes the posture of your heart because it keeps you in a place of humility. It also keeps you from becoming self-righteous.

Prayer will cause you to depend on the power of God and not your own gifting, talent, or strength. Prayer is the only way to have an intimate relationship with God.

> *And he spake a parable unto them to this end,*
> *that men ought always to pray, and not to faint;*
> Luke 18:1

Prayer is the key to the heart of God. It is also a place where He gives you revelation of the scriptures that you study about Him. Prayer completes the inner void in the soul of man: that place where cars, homes, land, or money can't fill.

> *For what shall it profit a man,*
> *if he shall gain the whole world, and lose his own soul?*
> Mark 8:36

Prayer is the one thing that gives the power to withstand temptation.

> *Watch ye and pray, lest ye enter into temptation.*
> *The spirit truly is ready, but the flesh is weak.*
> Mark 14:38

Fleshly lusts are tempting, but never put confidence in the flesh.

> *For I know that in me (that is, in my flesh,)*
> *dwelleth no good thing: for to will is present with me;*
> *but how to perform that which is good I find not.*
> Romans 7:18

To attempt to stand on your own fleshly ability and knowledge without a consistent prayer life would be equivalent to building your house upon sand.

> *And every one that heareth these sayings of mine, and doeth them*
> *not, shall be likened unto a foolish man, which built his house upon*
> *the sand: And the rain descended, and the floods came, and the*
> *winds blew, and beat upon that house; and it fell:*
> *and great was the fall of it.*
> Matthew 7:26-27

Prayer is the key to reach the heart of God.

> *And Samson called unto the Lord, and said,*
> *O Lord God, remember me, I pray thee, and strengthen me,*
> *I pray thee, only this once, O God, that I may be at once*
> *avenged of the Philistines for my two eyes.*
> Judges 16:28

When Samson prayed out of his own sincere heart, it pricked the heart of God to send help Samson's way. When you allow the enemy to shut down your prayer life, you are operating without spiritual eyes, and you will soon fall prey to temptation.

> *Confess your faults one to another, and pray one for another,*
> *that ye may be healed. The effectual fervent prayer*
> *of a righteous man availeth much.*
> James 5:16

God doesn't honor your prayers or accept your offerings if you have unforgiveness in your heart. If you cannot forgive others, God cannot forgive you.

> *Leave there thy gift before the altar, and go thy way; first be*
> *reconciled to thy brother, and then come and offer thy gift.*
> Matthew 5:24

> *And when ye stand praying, forgive,*
> *if ye have ought against any: that your Father also which is in*
> *heaven may forgive you your trespasses.*
> Mark 11:25

Your healing whether physical, spiritual, mental, or emotional begins with forgiveness and sincere prayer to unlock healing from God. It takes discipline to walk in a consistent lifestyle of prayer as much as it would to develop a consistent lifestyle of fasting, but it is a lifestyle worth developing. We can all pray a little more than we do. When you see that you have strayed from praying like you should, don't hesitate to get back to it. Prayer is not just you talking to God; there will be times when you just need to meditate on the Word of God and allow God to speak through His Word into your spirit. You will get more out of prayer when you view it as the most important time in your day. Prayer is one of the most important things in a Christian's life because it keeps him or her focused and aware of the nudging of the Holy Spirit and the ongoing spiritual warfare in the spirit realm. When you get too busy to pray, your soul gets restless and cannot be satisfied with carnal or tangible things. Developing a prayer lifestyle is important to the process of becoming a great leader because it is through prayer and meditation that you will receive direction from God. Through continual prayer, you will receive the necessary wisdom to modify your lifestyle according to your chosen purpose in the Kingdom of God.

CHAPTER 7

SPIRITUAL DIET

After forty days of fasting in the wilderness, the devil tempted Jesus who was hungry. Satan told Jesus to turn the stones into bread if He was the son of God. But Jesus wasn't buying that lie:

But he answered and said, It is written, Man shall not live by bread alone, but by every word that proceedeth out of the mouth of God.
Matthew 4:4

This is a powerful scripture because it deals with something that we do every day and like to do every day: eat! If we are not careful, spiritual hunger can be misdirected to physical hunger and turn into one of seven deadly sins (gluttony). More than one-third of adults in the United States are clinically obese. Gluttony has caused an epidemic of related health concerns: heart disease, stroke, cancer, diabetes, high blood pressure, high cholesterol, etc. The enemy will use any tool he can to keep us from maximizing our lives and fulfilling God's purpose for us. We should be mindful and deliberate in what we eat, what time we eat, and how much we eat so that we do not let the devil impact our effectiveness for the kingdom. Without good health, we are of limited use in how we serve the Lord.

We are all called to be witnesses for Jesus. To be an effective witness, we must be students of His Word.

Study to shew thyself approved unto God, a workman that needeth not to be ashamed, rightly dividing the word of truth.
II Timothy 2:15

So then faith cometh by hearing, and hearing by the word of God.
Romans 10:17

You must submit yourself to be taught so that your spiritual man can be fed. by the content in which it receives through the ear gate.

How then shall they call on him in whom they have not believed? and how shall they believe in him of whom they have not heard? and how shall they hear without a preacher?
Romans 10:14

Your spiritual diet is connected to the preacher, in the same way as the life of the branch comes from the vine.

I am the vine, ye are the branches: He that abideth in me, and I in him, the same bringeth forth much fruit: for without me ye can do nothing.
John 15:5

Your natural ear is the portal or mouth that feeds the spirit man.

He that hath an ear, let him hear what the Spirit saith unto the churches; To him that overcometh will I give to eat of the tree of life, which is in the midst of the paradise of God.
Revelation 2:7

There is a saying that you are what you eat. I say, you are led by what you digest into your spirit.

The steps of a good man are ordered by the Lord: and he delighteth in his way.
Psalm 37-23

The steps of a good man are a clear response to his spiritual diet. This verse is saying that you follow the direction of the spirit that you are influenced by. When a person is under the influence of negative spirits, his or her conduct will be negative. Negative spirits cause people to murder, rape, steal, and commit adultery. Thus, you must be guided by the Word of God and allow the Word to guide your actions

> *Finally, brethren, whatsoever things are true, whatsoever things are honest, whatsoever things are just, whatsoever things are pure, whatsoever things are lovely, whatsoever things are of good report; if there be any virtue, and if there be any praise, think on these things.*
> Philippians 4:8

Becoming a great leader starts with your thought life. You must permit the Word of God to guide your thoughts so that your actions will reflect that He is alive in you. Your diet reflects what you eat. Your actions reflect what you think.

> *Ye are the light of the world. A city that is set on an hill cannot be hid. Neither do men light a candle, and put it under a bushel, but on a candlestick; and it giveth light unto all that are in the house. Let your light so shine before men, that they may see your good works, and glorify your Father which is in heaven.*
> Matthew 5:14-16

Light bulbs are used to light up the darkness. There is no use in having a light bulb in a fixture and not turn the power on. Light bulbs shine differently according to the wattage of the bulb. Your mind is the bulb, the Word of God is the electricity - the more you read and study the Word of God, the brighter His light will reflect in your actions until it becomes so strong within you that it's magnified like a city set on a hill.

> *This book of the law shall not depart out of thy mouth; but thou shalt meditate therein day and night, that thou mayest observe to do according to all that is written therein: for then thou shalt make thy way prosperous, and then thou shalt have good success.*
> Joshua 1:8

How too often do we find ourselves studying our problems and rehearsing our frustrations in our minds, only to find that it brings more frustration adding to the problem instead of bringing peace to it? Continual study of the Word of God will shed light on every problem. Read the Word of God and bring every thought under subjection.

> *(For the weapons of our warfare are not carnal, but mighty through God to the pulling down of strong holds;)*
> *⁵ Casting down imaginations, and every high thing that exalteth itself against the knowledge of God, and bringing into captivity every thought to the obedience of Christ;*
> II Corinthians 10:4-5

Without a consistent diet of the Word of God, your thoughts and imaginations will take control of your life and become strongholds blocking your spiritual growth, keeping you in a cocoon-like state.

CHAPTER 8

HUMILITY

Humility begins when you realize that who you are, what you do, what you own, and what you know don't matter. Humility begins with your willingness to be rent asunder or bankrupted from a mindset that you are valued by your intellect and the things you possess. A great Bible example of this is Saul, (later named Paul). He was educated as a youth and later became a respected Pharisee who persecuted Christians. In Philippians 3, Paul modeled humility when he explained that he counted all his accomplishments as dung compared to the Gospel of Christ. He found out he just thought he had been righteous. He was proud and self-righteous, but all his pious grandstanding and structured observances and rituals were under the Law of Moses. They didn't mean anything compared to the righteousness of Christ and His free gift of grace. Righteousness through Christ had no rituals, it came to the believer by faith.

Paul's transformation began when he was on the road to Damascus. He was headed out to persecute some more Christians. Suddenly a great light shone around him that knocked him to the ground. He was blinded, but he was listening when he heard the voice of Christ ask him

… "Saul, Saul, why are you persecuting Me?"
Acts 9:4

God had to knock Saul down and blind him to get his attention. Does that sound familiar? Do you sometimes need God to hit you with a brick to get your attention? Saul was full of pride and self-righteousness at first, but after his conversion, God transformed Paul's mindset so that he realized that all he was before he met Christ didn't amount to a hill of beans and was meaningless in the Kingdom of God.

> *The sacrifices of God are a broken spirit: a broken and a contrite heart, O God, thou wilt not despise.*
> Psalm 51:17

Walking in humility involves having a broken spirit in the eyes of God which comes as a result of laying down ourselves for the cause of Christ and letting the Word of God break us so that we place God and the cause of Christ above our flesh. God is real and active in the lives of Christians. He searches our hearts and He checks us through the leadings and promptings of the Holy Spirit and through members of the body of Christ. If we obey and stay humble to the call, God will give us more than enough grace to reach those who are assigned to our lives. In the process of walking in humility, we develop Christian character.

When Paul embraced humility, his characteristics were shifted from the murderer Saul who carried the martyr Steven's coat while he was stoned, to Paul, a carrier of the gospel of Jesus Christ. Because of his willingness to be broken in the eyes of God, God took Saul's life as a Pharisee and transformed it to the life of the now-Christian Paul, who went on to write approximately two-thirds of the New Testament. God can use anyone regardless of past sin.

Like the five loaves and two fishes that fed the five thousand plus women and children, little is much when broken in the hands of Jesus. Such was the life of Apostle Paul. As a result of his brokenness, millions of people were able to receive spiritual food from a life sacrificed and broken for God's purposes.

Humility is one of the key requirements for and a great indicator of development of Christian character. Paul said,

> *I am crucified with Christ: nevertheless I live; yet not I, but Christ liveth in me: and the life which I now live in the flesh I live by the faith of the Son of God, who loved me, and gave himself for me.*
> Galatians 2:20

That became Paul's motto. Apostle Paul embraced the life of Christ as an example and standard of how we should conduct ourselves while living in this world. Thus, humility is so important that one can say development of Christian character shall not, will not, and cannot be acquired without it. It would be like trying to make a cake without a rising agent. It would never rise to the perfect level.

Jesus demonstrated humility. Though being part of the Triune Godhead, He humbled himself and took a lowly human form, walked among men, and suffered a humiliating crucifixion on the cross to save humanity. Jesus had the authority to speak and a legion of angels would have come to His aid but He chose to humble himself to the will of God the Father so that God's purpose for Him could be accomplished. Christ came disguised in human form as a servant to the human race to bring salvation to His creation. He humbled himself and became obedient unto death on the Cross.

To develop Christian character, we must learn to step down and let the teachings of Christ and the guidance of the Spirit of God through His Word, and Godly leadership, take precedence in our lives. We have to adopt the mind of Christ if we are to experience spiritual transformation, which is a humbling process in itself.

Philippians 2:5-9 says:

> *Let this mind be in you, which was also in Christ Jesus:*
> *⁶Who, being in the form of God, thought it not robbery to be equal with God:*
> *⁷ But made himself of no reputation, and took upon him the form of a servant, and was made in the likeness of men: And being found in*

> *fashion as a man, he humbled himself, and became obedient unto death, even the death of the cross.*
> *⁹ Wherefore God also hath highly exalted him, and given him a name which is above every name:*

Notice how the biblical perspective on humility differs from the worldly view, which sees humility as a sign of weakness. Unlike the worldly view, in the Kingdom of God, humility marks the road to development of Christian character and fulfillment of purpose.

CHAPTER 9

SUBMISSION

There is a mold, a blueprint, a map, or a road that everyone has to use to shape something, to build something, to find an address, or to travel upon. I want to use the word *submission* because in some way, everything had to submit in a fashion before it came to fruition.

Remember them which have the rule over you, who have spoken unto you the word of God: whose faith follow, considering the end of their conversation.

Hebrews 13:7

Obey them that have the rule over you, and submit yourselves: for they watch for your souls, as they that must give account, that they may do it with joy, and not with grief: for that is unprofitable for you.
Hebrews 13:17

God doesn't elevate you because you are perfect, but your elevation will come because you were willing to walk in humility. If you desire to become a great leader, you must be willing to submit to your visionary and to his vision as he follows the leading of God.

Those that be planted in the house of the Lord shall flourish in the courts of our God.
[14] They shall still bring forth fruit in old age; they shall be fat and flourishing.
Psalm 92:13-14

SUBMISSION

Your journey to greatness will begin through submission.

Abide in me, and I in you. As the branch cannot bear fruit of itself, except it abide in the vine; no more can ye, except ye abide in me.
John 15:4

The branch must remain connected to the vine to bring forth fruit, and greatness cannot be obtained without submission. Your actions can produce something that your heart does not submit to. If your heart is not in submission to the vision of your leader, you can't receive that which rests upon him. You must be in total submission willingly with the right attitude.

Likewise, ye younger, submit yourselves unto the elder. Yea, all of you be subject one to another, and be clothed with humility: for God resisteth the proud, and giveth grace to the humble. Humble yourselves therefore under the mighty hand of God, that he may exalt you in due time:
I Peter 5:5-6

We were created to serve but on different levels and in different ways. Your service is a sign of submission, but if you have a hidden motive while you are serving, you want to receive benefits for your efforts. It is vital that your heart is submitted to the Lord while you are serving at all times. This the key to keeping the right attitude. You don't get to choose whether to have the right attitude, even if you don't agree with how your leader is leading. You're on an assignment from God to serve with the right attitude and motives, even if you feel rejected, overlooked, unappreciated, or used. Serve with excellence as unto God. Submission is laying aside all you know to learn how to serve and flow in someone else's vision. Submission comes from a sweet spirit of cooperation that stems from trust. You must trust that your leader has your best interests at heart. When you don't trust your leader, you are not in total submission to them. God is your ultimate leader, remain in submission to Him.

Broken but Not Destroyed

*And Jesus took the loaves; and when he had given thanks,
he distributed to the disciples, and the disciples to them that were set
down; and likewise of the fishes as much as they would. When they
were filled, he said unto his disciples, Gather up the fragments that
remain, that nothing be lost. Therefore they gathered them together,
and filled twelve baskets with the fragments of the five barley loaves,
which remained over and above unto them that had eaten.*
John 6:11-13

Our lives are similar to the bread that Jesus blessed and broke to feed the five thousand. When we are thankful and submitted where we are, God will elevate and promote us. The twelve baskets represent your willingness to submit totally to the vision of your pastor, and it says because you allowed me to break you, you are now entering a season of more than enough, and your latter will be greater than the former. Your voice will still be speaking after you have left this world because you chose to totally submit to another's vision.

*The sacrifices of God are a broken spirit: a broken and a contrite
heart, O God, thou wilt not despise.*
Psalm 51:17

*I beseech you therefore, brethren, by the mercies of God,
that ye present your bodies a living sacrifice, holy, acceptable unto
God, which is your reasonable service.*
Romans 12:1

Like a seed that must first be submitted to the ground before a harvest will appear, there will be no harvest from your life without your willingness to make many sacrifices. Like an athlete who keeps his body under submission, greatness can never be accomplished in the Kingdom of God without many sacrifices.

SUBMISSION

Submission is often misunderstood, defining a person in the natural sense as weak or a pushover. In God's Kingdom, true submission shows you are mature, strong, and ready for the next level in God's plan for your life. Submission can also be viewed as a dirty word because of the way a true leader appears when he or she is truly submitted to a leader. Submission will often cause you to leave familiar surroundings. Every seed must leave its familiar place before it can grow. A grain of corn has to be separated from the cob, an acorn has to fall from the mighty oak tree before it can grow and become a mighty oak in its own right.

*Now the Lord had said unto Abram,
Get thee out of thy country, and from thy kindred, and from thy father's house, unto a land that I will shew thee:*
Genesis 12:1

Abraham had to sacrifice by leaving his homeland, Mesopotamia, which was between the Tigris and Euphrates Rivers, what is modern day Iraq and Iran. The climate was hot and dry, perfect for farming barley, and sesame. When the land flooded from the rivers, rich soil was left behind and there were beautiful green meadows which made raising livestock easy. It was a huge sacrifice that Abraham made by turning his back on a land as rich and abundant as Mesopotamia.

When God calls you out, it will in no wise look right to your human perspective. A Godly call can't be comprehended by the carnal mind.

*Now faith is the substance of things hoped for,
the evidence of things not seen.*
Hebrews 11:1

Faith doesn't respond by what it can see, it obeys and moves in the direction in which God instructs.

> *And the Lord said unto Abram,*
> *after that Lot was separated from him, Lift up now thine eyes,*
> *and look from the place where thou art northward, and southward,*
> *and eastward, and westward: For all the land which thou seest,*
> *to thee will I give it, and to thy seed for ever.*
> Genesis 13:14-15

It would be great if family could be around during the process God takes you through as a leader but in many cases, there will be a season when you must separate from family. It's not enough just to leave your homeland, God wants you to turn your heart from it. When your heart is turned from it, then He can then give you the promise, but you must believe that what's in front of you is far greater than that which you are leaving behind. If you turn back to the connections in your past life, you are like Lot's wife. She was so insignificant that her name isn't even mentioned in the Bible. When she looked back regretting the things she would lose, she was turned to pillar of salt. Her remains are said to still stand as a testimony to her willful defiance and disobedience to God.

When a seed is planted in the earth, it has no choice in the matter. It can't go against God's Law. It must submit to the ground, decay, and die, losing its exterior covering before it can bring forth fruit.

Submission is more about the attitude that you have while under the authority of another visionary, while obedience is an action that can be carried out without having the right attitude. You can be obedient and still have a terrible attitude, but you can't receive a greater anointing or become a great leader without the right attitude. Submission is a form of death because it literally means to bow, defer, yield, give ground, buckle, capitulate, succumb, surrender, fold, turn in. (Yield, n.d.)

SUBMISSION

*Verily, verily, I say unto you, Except a corn of wheat fall into the
ground and die, it abideth alone: but if it die,
it bringeth forth much fruit.*
John 12:24

If it dies, it produces many seeds. Until you submit unto death in someone else's vision, that vision which lies dormant in you will never come to life or grow to fruition

Chapter 10

Spiritual Control

Many people who attempt to get their lives together without Christ eventually realize that it cannot be done by self efforts. Self-control can only be obtained through the Spirit of God, which is the only way the body and mind can come under subjection.

Watch and pray, that ye enter not into temptation: the spirit indeed is willing, but the flesh is weak.
Matthew 26:41

Our spirit as Christians is subject to and comes from God and will always be willing to do the things that are right in the eyes of God. However, our flesh is fallen and is subject to sin and death. Thus, if you are operating in the flesh, we cannot please God.

*For to be carnally minded is death;
but to be spiritually minded is life and peace.*
Romans 8:6

Paul describes his struggle with his flesh in Romans 7:18-23 saying,

For I know that in me (that is, in my flesh,) dwelleth no good thing: for to will is present with me; but how to perform that which is good I find not. For the good that I would I do not: but the evil which I would not, that I do. Now if I do that I would not, it is no more I that do it, but sin that dwelleth in me. I find then a law, that, when I would do good, evil is present with me. For I delight in the law of God after the inward man: But I see another law in my members, warring against the law of my mind, and bringing me into captivity to the law of sin which is in my members.

The only way we can win this war is through Spirit-controlled life which begins with having a sober mind whose thought life that is guided by the Word of God, giving superior guidelines. There are many desires of the flesh that can cause us to stumble in life. According to Galatians 5:19-20, they include adultery, fornication, uncleanness, lasciviousness, idolatry, witchcraft, hatred, wrath, strife, sedition, heresies, envying, murders, drunkenness and reveling. Thus, one must

Be sober, be vigilant; because your adversary the devil, as a roaring lion, walketh about, seeking whom he may devour:
I Peter 5:8

Once we give our lives to Christ, we must forbid our previous appetites, the impressions we used to allow upon, our senses, the satisfactions we sought which were ungodly, and the activities of the flesh we engaged in to continue in this fearfully and wonderfully made instrument, which we are in God. Our bodies must now be controlled according to God's standards. Paul writes in Galatians 6:8 that if you pursue carnality, your outcome will be corruption, and goes further to say in I Corinthians 9:17 that we must put our bodies under subjection and stop sewing to the flesh. The body is a good servant but a bad master.

The Bible shows us how our flesh, if left unchecked, can easily lead us to sin. II Samuel 11 contains the story of King David and Bathsheba. David arose up one morning and took a walk around the roof of his palace. They walked on flat roofs a lot in Israel. From the rooftop, he saw a beautiful woman bathing herself. David sent someone to inquire about the woman and he found out that her name was Bathsheba, the daughter of Eliam, and her husband was Uriah. Instead of David using spiritual control, he was consumed with his lust for Bathsheba. Uriah was a soldier at war fighting with David's men. David should have stopped when he found out that she was Uriah's wife but instead David sent for Bathsheba and slept with her. She got pregnant. David had to try to cover up his sin so he sent for Uriah and told him to go and be with his wife. However, Uriah was a faithful soldier and refused a conjugal visit because his men did not get to come home, so he was not going to take advantage of the situation. David had Uriah murdered by sending him to the front line of the hottest battle. In this story, envy filled David's heart, followed by lust, which led him to adultery then murder to cover up the sin. David was a great king but he almost lost his entire kingdom because of his great sin. Through the life of David, we can see how flesh if not checked can lead us to sin and destruction. Dr. Charles Stanley often says that sin takes you further than you want to go and keeps you longer than you want to stay.

Another account is that of Samson in Judges 16. Samson was born a Nazarene. He understood that he couldn't drink wine or cut his hair; neither could he marry a Philistine woman. The rules were taught to him by his parents from his youth. His restrictions challenged him and he continually walked in disobedience. Samson failed to exercise spiritual control, neither did he live a life as a Nazarite, although he was permanently slated. Samson's life was out of control and under the control of his flesh. He was to abstain from anything fermented, grapes, raisins, even grape juice. But Samson broke his vows while passing by the vineyards of Timnah. Samson was arrogant and often walked right into temptation. Samson willingly walked into conditions that would lead any human to unrighteousness, but each time God was merciful and pulled him out. Each time Samson disobeyed, it brought him closer to death. He did not have spiritual control and did not honor his mother or father, and because of this, his days were cut short.

Another somewhat similar example is the account of Joseph and Potiphar's wife in Genesis 39. Joseph was favored above his brothers because he was the son of his father's old age. Joseph's life gives an extraordinary display of spiritual control. Joseph was thrown into a pit by his brothers, kidnapped, and sold into slavery but he never sought revenge. Joseph was a handsome young man as well as very intelligent.

He honored God and everything he put his hands to prospered because God was with him. When Potiphar's wife laid her eyes on Joseph, she was infatuated with him, and as time went by, she began asking him to lie with her. Joseph would not give in to her because he feared God. He also respected his relationship with Potiphar. When the opportunity came and she was alone with him, she threw herself at Joseph to entice him. He had to run but he left his garment, and she tore it. She accused him of rape. Joseph was thrown into prison but he still held onto his integrity. Joseph exemplified spiritual control throughout his entire life, and as a result, God's blessings were always upon him. Joseph was given uncommon favor because of his spiritual control and discipline to the Holy Spirit. Thus, from this biblical account, we see the importance of learning spiritual control because it is development of Christian character.

Apostle Paul also reflected spiritual control after he was converted. A great part of Paul's writing was done while he was in prison. In Paul's time, prisons were used to hold people accused of crimes rather than punishing them for breaking the law. Prison is a place of many challenges, but Paul had spiritual control. Because of his relationship with God, instead of worrying, he wrote to the Ephesians, Philippians, Colossians, and Philemon. Even though incarcerated, he remained grateful in all circumstances. The average person might lose their mind or hope if in Paul's circumstances. The Bible says that Paul endured more than just prison:

> *Of the Jews five times received I forty stripes save one. Thrice was I beaten with rods, once was I stoned, thrice I suffered shipwreck, a night and a day I have been in the deep; In journeyings often, in perils of waters, in perils of robbers, in perils by mine own countrymen, in perils by the heathen, in perils in the city, in perils in the wilderness, in perils in the sea, in perils among false brethren; In weariness and painfulness, in watchings often, in hunger and thirst, in fastings often, in cold and nakedness.*
> II Corinthians 11:24-27

Through it all, Paul was able to stay in control because he trusted the Spirit of God. He was definitely sold out for the purpose of reaching as many as he could through his writing. I believe that what he endured would have caused many in today's world to lose faith and quit. Yet Paul continued walking in spiritual control and stayed faithful to the calling on his life and faithful to God.

Jesus is the best example of spiritual control. He was the fulfillment of all that was spoken of by the prophets. He came wrapped in human form. Jesus could have come to the earth as a king. He made no reputation for Himself, but He became obedient unto death, even the death of the cross. In the of Garden Gethsemane, Jesus prayed until it was as great drops of blood flowing from His face, and was overwhelmed by the thought of what would happen to Him.

And he went a little farther, and fell on his face, and prayed, saying, O my Father, if it be possible, let this cup pass from me: nevertheless not as I will, but as thou wilt.
Matthew 26:39

Jesus had foreseen the betrayal, ridicule, and pain He would experience. Jesus fulfilled what was foretold of Him by the prophet Isaiah in the Old Testament.

But he was wounded for our transgressions, he was bruised for our iniquities: the chastisement of our peace was upon him; and with his stripes we are healed.
Isaiah 53:5

Jesus lived a spiritually-controlled life to leave us with much hope that it can be done. When Jesus was in the wilderness forty days and forty nights without food or water, he felt hunger pains. Satan came and tested him at his moment of weakness and said,

> *And when the tempter came to him, he said, If thou be the Son of God, command that these stones be made bread.*
> Matthew 4:3

Jesus resisted Satan by quoting the Word of God saying

> *But he answered and said, It is written, Man shall not live by bread alone, but by every word that proceedeth out of the mouth of God.*
> Matthew 4:4

Spiritual control starts with studying and knowing your rights according to the Word of God and living a lifestyle in alignment to the Holy Scripture. You must learn to use the Word of God against the enemy when he launches an attack in your mind. We are human sinners, but we can look to Jesus as the perfect example of Christian character and self-control.

> *Looking unto Jesus the author and finisher of our faith; who for the joy that was set before him endured the cross, despising the shame, and is set down at the right hand of the throne of God.*
> Hebrews 12:2

CHAPTER 11

PUSH!

The process which prepares you to be a great leader all comes down to your *spiritual push*. I took the idea of spiritual push from two scriptures. The first was

If ye be willing and obedient, ye shall eat the good of the land:
Isaiah 1:19

and the second was

Submit yourselves therefore to God. Resist the devil, and he will flee from you.
James 4:7

There are two words in each verse that have significance. The first words are *willing* coupled with *obedient*. The widow woman was from Zarephath was "pushed" into a place of "more than enough" because she was willing to obey and submit her will to God, which gave her the power to resist fixing her last bit of meal, and using the last of her oil on herself but instead fed the prophet Elijah. The second set of words include *resist* and *submit*. Your power to resist comes from your willingness to submit. When looking at these words, they are designed to push you into your destined place in the Kingdom of God. Walking by the spiritual meaning of these words is what will give you the spiritual push you need to move closer to God.

And Ruth said, Intreat me not to leave thee, or to return from following after thee: for whither thou goest, I will go; and where thou lodgest, I will lodge: thy people shall be my people, and thy God my God.
Ruth 1:16

Ruth was willing to leave her homeland and come under the obedience of the God of Naomi, submitting herself to Him and resisting the temptation presented by the enemy to turn back to the familiar. Ruth's spiritual push was activated by her willingness, obedience, submission, and resistance. God rewarded her submission and attitude of obedience by thrusting her into the field of Boaz. By resisting the devil, she was pushed into a place ownership.

It doesn't feel good at times to be attentive, obedient, and submissive to God, and it can be a challenge at times to resist the many temptations presented by the devil. But every time you do you, are pushed closer to your destined place in the Kingdom of God.

Rejection is a form of push. After a woman has carried a baby for nine months, the body begins to reject what it once nurtured. The body begins to reject the baby because it has outgrown the womb and is now ready to experience another world.

He is despised and rejected of men; a man of sorrows, and acquainted with grief: and we hid as it were our faces from him; he was despised, and we esteemed him not.
Isaiah 53:3

After Jesus had finished his assignment on earth, the world wasn't big enough for him any longer. It then began to reject Him. In the same way, when you have outgrown a certain area in ministry, you will also experience rejection. Rejection is like Pitocin, a synthetic form of oxytocin, used to induce labor. Rejection is a sign that you have outgrown the current position. Rejection puts you in the spiritual birth canal on your way to another dimension in the Kingdom of God. Rejection is the part in your process that pushes you in the direction of your destined place in the Kingdom of God. Joseph's rejection from his family pushed him into his destiny as Pharaoh's second-in-command.

When an eagle's chicks are old enough to survive, the mother eagle begins to reject them, making things uncomfortable for them. Then she pushes them out of the nest. It appears that she is killing her chicks by doing this, but without the push, the chicks' wing muscles would never be strengthened. Rejection is not designed to kill you, but to push you out of your comfort zone so that you will spread your wings and learn to fly on your own. David would have never become the king that he was if Saul had not rejected him.

Struggle simply means it will require some sort of effort, whether difficult are not. Whenever you think about getting in shape and eating right, you automatically understand that there will be a struggle and without it, you will remain in the same state. Without the struggle, there would be no strength. Without the struggle, victory would have no meaning. In fact, during the struggle you gain the tools needed to learn and accept responsibility. We live in a generation that doesn't understand the importance of struggle, but rather has a sense of entitlement. Many people want influence, power, and prestige without putting in work. It is the struggles of life that bring pain with a smile. Giving birth to a child is a severe struggle for the mother but the same struggle brings a smile only moments later. When running in a race, the body feels weary because of the struggle but afterward, the reward is exhilarating. Our strength is in the struggle as Samson's strength was in his hair. But when there is no struggle our spiritual hair can't grow, leaving us blind and weak spiritually. Samson needed to experience the weight of the fetters of brass, smell the stink of the prison, and feel the struggle of grinding mill because in the midst of his struggle, his hair began to grow back and no one paid attention.

Embrace your struggles.

> *My brethren, count it all joy when ye fall into divers temptations;*
> *Knowing this, that the trying of your faith worketh patience.*
> *But let patience have her perfect work, that ye may be*
> *perfect and entire, wanting nothing.*
> James 1:2-4

It is your struggles that push away laziness, selfishness, and teach you compassion. Many spend thousands of the hard-earned dollars to hit the Powerball trying to avoid the struggle of earning a living. Struggle has more value than their money because it is the tool that will help you hold onto things that you would normally consider useless. It is your struggle and failures that reflect the beauty hidden within.

> *And let us not be weary in well doing:*
> *for in due season we shall reap, if we faint not.*
> Galatians 6:9

Everything you have gone through up until now all comes down to your willingness to push. As men and women of God, you must understand that the darkest hour is just before the day. It may take years before God pushes you into your destiny. Your attitude and willingness to submit will determine how long. The enemy will always launch his fiercest attack before you enter your assignment as a great leader and right after you are seated in your position. When you begin to experience a flood of tests and trials one after the next, that is your sign to PUSH!

When you push, there will be pressure, pain, stumbling blocks, and problems in the process of your birthing as a leader. Experience the struggle and count it all joy, for it is your struggles in life that strengthen you to be the effective leader that God made you to be.

> *I press toward the mark for the prize*
> *of the high calling of God in Christ Jesus.*
> Philippians 3:14

REFERENCES

Barnes, A. (1947). *Notes, explanatory and practical, on the second epistle to the Corinthians and the epistle to the Galatians.* (p. 55). New York, NY: Harper & Brothers.

Black hole. (2017, February 14). Retrieved February 12, 2017, from https://en.wikipedia.org/wiki/Black_hole

Clarke, A., & Smith, T. (1875). *The Holy Bible, containing the Old and New Testament: (Authorized translation), including the marginal readings and parallel texts.* (p. 1334). London: Tegg.

Pastor Burnout Statistics. (n.d.). Retrieved February 13, 2017, from http://www.pastorburnout.com/pastor-burnout-statistics.html

Rankin, L. (2015). *Mind over medicine: scientific proof that you can heal yourself.* Brighton-Le-Sands, NSW: Hay House Australia Pty Ltd.

Yield. (n.d.). Retrieved February 18, 2017, from http://www.thefreedictionary.com/yield

Your Mind Can Make You Sick. (n.d.). Retrieved February 12, 2017, from http://www.gilead.net/health/mindsick.html

8, 2. K. (n.d.). The Power Of A Vision. Retrieved February 13, 2017, from https://jesusculture.com/posts/1450-the-power-of-a-vision/

Note from the Publisher

Are you a first time author?

Not sure how to proceed to get your book published?
Want to keep all your rights and all your royalties?
Want it to look as good as a Top 10 publisher?
Need help with editing, layout, cover design?
Want it out there selling in 90 days or less?

Visit our website for some exciting new options!

www.chalfant-eckert-publishing.com

www.ingramcontent.com/pod-product-compliance
Lightning Source LLC
LaVergne TN
LVHW051511070426
835507LV00022B/3046